Accessing ... Citizenship: Crime and Justice

Teacher Guide
Special Educational Needs

Bhavini Algarra

© 2004 Folens Limited, on behalf of the author.

United Kingdom: Folens Publishers, Apex Business Centre, Boscombe Road, Dunstable, LU5 4RL.
Email: folens@folens.com

Ireland: Folens Publishers, Greenhills Road, Tallaght, Dublin 24.
Email: info@folens.ie

Poland: JUKA, ul. Renesansowa 38, Warsaw 01-905.

Folens allows photocopying of pages marked 'copiable page' for educational use, providing that this use is within the confines of the purchasing institution. Copiable pages should not be declared in any return in respect of photocopying licence. Folens publications are protected by international copyright laws. All rights are reserved. The copyright of all materials in this publication, except where otherwise stated,remains the property of the publisher and authors. No part of this publication may be reproduced, stored in a retrieval system, or transmitted, in any form or by any means, for whatever purpose, without the written permission of Folens Limited.

Bhavini Algarra hereby asserts her moral right to be identified as the author of this work in accordance with the Copyright, Designs and Patents Act 1988.

Editor: Louise Titley
Layout artist: Kim Sillitoe
Cover design: 2i Design
Page design: Darren Watts
Illustrations: Ray and Corinne Burrows and Dave Thompson, Beehive Illustration

First published 2004 by Folens Limited.

Every effort has been made to contact copyright holders of material used in this publication. If any copyright holder has been overlooked, we should be pleased to make any necessary arrangements.

British Library Cataloguing in Publication Data. A catalogue record for this publication is available from the British Library.

ISBN 1 84303 569 3

Contents

Teacher notes   4

Law and Order

Why do we have laws?	6
Criminal acts … who's breaking the law?	8
Criminal law and civil law … what's the difference?	9
'I'll see you in court!' … But which one?	12

Policing

Policing today	15
Reducing crime … focus on Stop and Search	16
Does crime pay?	18
What punishment?	20
Life behind bars	21

Crime and Punishment?

Anti-social behaviour orders … is this the way forward?	22
Is there justice?	25
The Howard League for Penal Reform	26
Is there an alternative? … Focus on Grendon Prison	28
The Youth Justice System	29

Preventing crime	30
Want to know more?	32

Teacher notes

On the photocopiable pages of the Teacher Guides in this series, the three different levels of ability are indicated by symbols in the heading at the top of the page: a triangle for special needs, a circle for mainstream and a square for gifted and talented.

Not all the activity pages have accompanying notes as many of the tasks are self-explanatory.

Why do we have laws?

Student Book: pp 4–5
Activity 1: What is happening?
Get the pupils to work in small groups. Assign an image to each group and ask them to discuss what is happening in the image. Then give the groups the activity sheet; you may want to enlarge it to A3 so all the group members can see the questions. The pupils complete the activity sheet and feed back their findings to the rest of the class. Record key words on the board.

Activity 2: What if it were really true?
The children should work individually or in pairs. Read the statement in the middle of the page. Explain who the anarchists are, what they want and how they want the country to be 'governed'. You could get some of the pupils to share their ideas of what life would be like.

Other ideas
- Class collage: collect images to create one large class image of what life could be like if we didn't have any laws. Different groups could work on different ideas.

- Class discussion: ask pupils if they think laws are necessary. Pupils should be encouraged to offer reasons for their own views.

Criminal acts ... who's breaking the law?

Student Book: pp 6–7
Activity 1: Is it legal or illegal?
Once the groups have completed the table, read out the correct answers, which are as follows.

a Legal: the age at which you can buy alcohol is 18.
b Legal: the law only concerns purchasing alcohol and consuming it on licensed premises.
c Illegal.
d Illegal.
e Legal: provided it is a small tractor and the child is 16 years old.
f Illegal: you have to be 17 to drive a car.
g Legal: the age of consent is 16 years of age.
h Illegal.
i Legal.
j Illegal: you cannot buy pets until you are 12 years old.
k Illegal: tortoises are not allowed to be sold as pets.
l Illegal: although the response of the police may vary in different areas.
m Legal in licensed premises in the Netherlands.
n Illegal: this is theft.
o Illegal: this is fraud/theft.
p Illegal: this is burglary.

The maximum term for theft is 10 years imprisonment, for burglary 14 years, although violence can increase this term.

Criminal and civil law ... what's the difference?

Student Book: pp 8–9
Activity 1: The difference between criminal and civil law
The activities could be done individually or in pairs.

The correct sentences are:

1 Civil law deals with disputes between individuals and groups.
2 Areas covered by civil law include copyright issues, trespass or unfair dismissal.
3 A criminal offence is behaviour that breaks the laws of the country.
4 Criminal cases, like murder, are between the Crown Prosecution Service and the offender.
5 The main aim of a criminal prosecution is to punish the offender.

Activity 2: Examining the headlines
Ask the pupils to share which civil and criminal headlines interested them the most and give their reasons why.

Other ideas
- Class discussion: should newspapers highlight civil or criminal cases like the ones shown or should they remain 'private'?

Extension activity

Ask the pupils to find some more current examples of civil and/or criminal cases in the media.

'I'll see you in court!' ... But which one?

Student Book: pp 10–11

Activity 2: True or false?

Answers for the true or false statements are as follows:

1 True, **2** False, **3** True, **4** False, **5** True, **6** False, **7** True, **8** False, **9** True, **10** False, **11** True, **12** False

Policing today

Student Book: pp 12–13

See if it is possible to invite a police officer to school. Get the pupils to prepare questions on what it is like to be an officer and the different 'jobs' they have to do.

Reducing crime ... focus on Stop and Search

Student Book: pp 14–15

The various activities link to the concepts about police powers and the discretion they exercise in implementing them. The worksheets provide information to start a discussion in class about the nature of the practice and arguments about its effectiveness. The discussions should help to highlight both the importance of granting police sufficient powers to carry out their jobs and the difficulties involved when making judgements about how to implement those powers.

Does crime pay?

Student Book: pp 16–21

For pupils to be able to carry out the survey, you will need to leave one or two weeks between doing the survey and collating the findings, so that everyone has a chance to complete the task.

What punishment?

Student Book: pp 22–23

The word search answers are:

g	i	b	b	e	t	i	r	o	n	s	y	n	s
h	s	h	m	t	s	v	a	n	j	l	o	a	c
h	b	m	l	k	j	h	g	f	d	s	a	a
f	l	a	z	c	b	n	m	j	l	p	m	b	f
c	i	d	v	b	x	b	v	e	f	y	h	u	f
b	f	h	t	q	a	j	e	w	u	p	z	o
m	e	p	m	u	t	r	e	a	d	m	i	l	l
o	l	l	i	j	a	g	s	h	i	e	w	l	d
p	p	t	c	r	i	m	i	n	a	l	s	m	w
s	u	i	y	l	r	c	s	h	b	n	e	p	s
t	r	e	w	q	f	g	p	i	h	g	i	r	a
o	y	f	c	v	n	l	c	h	t	r	a	i	s
c	s	o	g	u	m	a	n	a	c	l	e	s	a
k	a	d	g	l	o	t	h	u	p	w	o	o	m
s	h	a	c	k	l	e	s	y	d	r	i	n	b
p	c	i	d	s	r	a	f	h	b	z	m	o	l
p	u	n	i	s	h	e	d	h	p	m	u	t	p

Extension activity

You could set an individual or group project looking at how punishments have changed through history.

Life behind bars

Student Book: pp 24–25

This is an empathy exercise to get pupils to think about what life might be like in prison. You could use extracts from novels or newspapers to give them some ideas, as well as discussing the photographs in the Student Book before doing the activity.

Anti-social behaviour orders ... is this the way forward?

Student Book: pp 26–27

This is a very controversial policy; use the information cards and activities to generate discussion about whether ASBOs are a good idea. How would the pupils feel if they were 'named and shamed' in their local area?

The Youth Justice System

Student Book: pp 38–39

Activity 1: What is happening?
Answers

1 Youth
2 Responsibility
3 Usher
4 Restoration
5 Health worker
6 Youth justice Board
7 Education worker
8 Social worker
9 Probation officer
10 Reintegration
11 Police officer
12 Home Secretary
13 Drugs
14 Young offenders' institution
15 Witness
16 Court
17 Boredom
18 Magistrate

6 Accessing ... Citizenship: Crime and Justice

Why do we have laws?

Activity 1: What is happening?

Words to describe what is happening in the photo from the Student Book we are discussing are:

Is the image positive or negative?

The title or headline we would give this image is:

The reasons why we have chosen this headline are:

© Folens (copiable page), Accessing ... Citizenship: Crime and Justice

Accessing ... Citizenship: Crime and Justice

Why do we have laws?

Activity 2: What if it were really true?

Imagine that the anarchists really have come to power and want to get rid of all the laws. What do you think would happen where you live if there weren't any laws?

Draw what you think life would be like ...

| Life tomorrow ... | Life in a week's time ... |

Now the anarchists have come to power, what happens next?

| Life in a month's time ... | Life in a year's time ... |

© Folens (copiable page), Accessing ... Citizenship: Crime and Justice

8 Accessing ... Citizenship: Crime and Justice

Criminal acts ... who's breaking the law?

Activity 1: Is it legal or illegal?

Work in pairs or small groups. Look at the examples given in the Student Book. Which examples are illegal? Which examples are legal? Write down underneath each letter whether you think the example is legal or illegal.

Legal means allowed by the law.		**Illegal** means against the law.	
a	b	c	d
e	f	g	h
i	j	k	l
m	n	o	p

Activity 2: How serious is it?

- Your teacher will give you the answers. How many did you get correct?
    1. Now cut out the squares and place the acts that are illegal in one pile and the acts that are legal in another pile.
    2. Now put the crimes in order of seriousness.
    3. Which crimes do you think should carry the stiffest sentences?
- You are going to tell the rest of the class what your group decided.

Remember to think about:
- The level of violence used or threatened.
- The number of previous crimes committed.
- How much planning was involved in the crime?
- The value of any goods taken.
- Who was the victim? Was it an individual, a business, a rich person or a poor person?

© Folens (copiable page), Accessing ... Citizenship: Crime and Justice

Criminal and civil law ... what's the difference?

Activity 1: The difference between criminal and civil law

Match the sentence beginning to the correct ending.

Sentence beginnings	link words	Sentence endings
1 Civil law deals with disputes	include	the laws of the country
2 Areas covered by civil law	between	individuals and groups
3 A criminal offence is behaviour that	is to	punish the offender
4 Criminal cases like murder are	breaks	copyright issues, trespass, unfair dismissal
5 The main aim of a criminal prosecution	between	the Crown Prosecution Service and the offender

Your teacher will give you the right endings when you have finished.

Activity 2: Examining the headlines

Look at the headlines in the Student Book on pages 8 and 9. Sort them into civil crimes or criminal crimes and give a reason why. Use the correct sentences from Activity 1 to help you.

Headline	Civil or criminal	Reason
1		
2		
3		
4		
5		
6		
7		
8		
9		
10		
11		

© Folens (copiable page), Accessing ... Citizenship: Crime and Justice

Criminal and civil law ... what's the difference?

Activity 3: Investigating a civil case

The civil headline which interests me most is ...

The reasons for my choice are ...

What would I like to find out about the case?

What questions would I ask?

Criminal and civil law ... what's the difference?

Activity 4: Investigating a criminal case

The criminal headline which interests me most is ...

The reasons for my choice are ...

What would I like to find out about the case?

What questions would I ask?

12 Accessing ... Citizenship: Crime and Justice

'I'll see you in court!' ... But which one?

Activity 1: Spot the difference!

List the differences you can see between the crown court and the magistrates' court shown in the Student Book on pages 10 and 11. Write your list on a clean sheet of paper.

Activity 2: True or false?

Use the information cards that your teacher will give you about the different courts to complete this activity.

		True or false?
1	You can become a magistrate without any experience or knowledge of the law.	
2	Only the most serious offences are heard in the magistrates' court.	
3	Most criminal cases are heard in a magistrates' court.	
4	Everyone in the magistrates' court has a trial by jury.	
5	Six months is the maximum sentence a magistrate can give.	
6	Magistrates have unlimited power to fine people.	
7	Most cases in a crown court are heard by a jury and judge.	
8	The judge decides whether the defendant is guilty.	
9	You can appeal against convictions in the crown court.	
10	There is a jury present during an appeal.	
11	The crown court will only deal with cases that seem to be more serious or important.	
12	The Yorkshire Ripper was tried in a magistrates' court.	

Once your teacher has told you the right answers, correct any that you got wrong so that you end up with twelve correct statements.

© Folens (copiable page), Accessing ... Citizenship: Crime and Justice

'I'll see you in court!'... But which one?

Information card 1: True or false?

- Most people who come in contact with the court system will do so at the magistrates' court.

- The types of cases heard in a magistrates' court vary from parking offences to assault.

- There usually at least two magistrates and not more than seven present in court. Magistrates are often not legally qualified and are not paid.

- Because magistrates are not lawyers, they have advice on the law from a court clerk.

- Most defendants plead guilty. The court then decides what sentence to give them. The maximum sentence a magistrate can give is six months in prison and/or a fine of no more than £20,000 for any one offence.

- The magistrate is there to make sure both sides to the proceedings act in accordance with the rules.

- A defendant who pleads not guilty can choose to go to a crown court for trial.

- The advantage of going to a crown court is that you get a trial by jury and this means you are more likely to be let off.

- Defendants who plead not guilty stand a 20% chance of being let off in a magistrates' court. In a crown court they have a 60% chance of being let off.

'I'll see you in court!' ... But which one?

Information card 2: True or false?

- The disadvantages of going to crown court are that the process takes longer, is more expensive, and carries the risk that the defendant will end up receiving a much higher sentence!

- The most famous crown court is the Old Bailey. Some of England's most famous cases have been tried there including the Yorkshire Ripper and the Soham murders.

- The crown court deals with all serious offences that can be tried before a judge and jury. These offences include murder, rape, serious assault, kidnapping, conspiracy, fraud, armed robbery, and breaking the Official Secrets Act. These offences cannot be tried at the magistrates' court.

- When there is a jury in court, the judge guides the jury, but the jury decide on their own in the jury room if the defendant is guilty or not.

- A jury is made up of 12 people aged between 18 and 70 taken from the electoral list. What goes on in the jury room is secret. The jury decides whether the defendant is guilty or not, by looking at the facts which have been discussed during the trial.

- About 25% of defendants plead not guilty.

- The crown court is also the place where people can appeal against convictions and sentences by magistrates. When listening to an appeal against conviction, the crown court judge re-hears all the evidence that witnesses have already given in the lower court, but there is no jury. For all appeals, the judge makes his or her decision with the help of between two and four magistrates.

Policing today

Activity 1: The many different faces of the police force

Look at the collage of photos in the Student Book on pages 12 and 13. Write a sentence describing what the police officers are doing in each of the different pictures.

Activity 2: What qualities do you need to become a police officer?

Complete the picture. What skills and qualities does a person need to become a police officer? Write down your ideas around the picture.

Reducing crime ... focus on Stop and Search

Activity 1: Why use Stop and Search?

> Why do you think the police would use Stop and Search?

Activity 2: Arguments for and against Stop and Search

Read through the following statements. Mark in RED the arguments against Stop and Search. Mark in BLUE the arguments for Stop and Search.

The police need the power to stop and search anyone they suspect of doing something wrong.	Stop and Search seems to cause more problems than it solves. Sometimes people are stopped for no clear reason. This makes them resentful.
A report singled out Stop and Search as one of the worst examples of 'institutional racism'.	Police who are trained in Stop and Search have to memorise ten rules to prevent conflict. These include: do not tell people to 'shut up' or 'stand still'; do not call people names and do not assume someone is guilty because they do not look you in the eye.
In one year, Stop and Search helped the Metropolitan Police solve more than 500 street robberies and over 1,000 burglaries.	There are guidelines in place which mean the police have to give a written report to anyone who is stopped and searched.
In 1986, 17% of Stop and Searches led to arrests. In 1998, this had fallen to only 8%.	Stop and Search makes would-be criminals think twice before they commit an offence. It cuts down on street robbery and the carrying of weapons.
Stop and Search leads to the arrest of one in four drug dealers.	Stop and Search has led to the arrest of some of the most dangerous terrorists of recent years.

Reducing crime ... focus on Stop and Search

Activity 3: Which arguments are the strongest?

Working with a partner, choose three of the most important arguments against Stop and Search. Next, choose the three most important arguments for Stop and Search. Then join with another pair to agree upon two of the most important arguments either for or against Stop and Search. Share your conclusions with the rest of the class. Don't forget to say how you decided which arguments you chose.

Activity 4: If you were in the park

Imagine you are the youth in the park shown in the Student Book on page 15.

1 What are the police officers saying to you?
2 How do you respond?
3 Complete the conversation you might be having with the police officers.
4 Continue your writing on a sheet of paper if you need extra space.

Accessing ... Citizenship: Crime and Justice

Does crime pay?

Activity 1: Do your own research

Working in pairs, ask 10 young people to complete the survey your teacher will give you. You could ask them to complete the survey and then return it to a collection box without giving their names.

Activity 2: What did you find out?

Once all the surveys have been returned, you need to look at all the findings. You could draw graphs like the ones shown in the Student Book and highlight key comments made in the survey. Share your findings with the rest of class. The teacher will make a note of everyone's findings on the board so you can get the 'complete picture' of the survey done by your class.

Activity 3: Were your class's findings similar to those in the Student Book?

What similarities did you have?

What differences did you have?

Did any of the findings in the Student Book surprise you?

Were you surprised by the findings of your class survey?

Did any of your findings surprise you particularly?

Why do you think so many newspapers around the country were keen to write about the survey's findings?

What do you think would be the best way to put young people off getting involved in crime?

Does crime pay?

The Survey: Does crime pay?

Please complete the following survey and return to _____
by (date) _____

1. Have you ever been a victim of crime?   Yes ☐   No ☐

2. If you have been a victim, what kind of crime?
   Assault ☐   Mugging ☐
   Theft ☐   Other ☐

3. Have you ever been involved in crime?   Yes ☐   No ☐

4. If you have been involved in crime, what kind of crime was it?
   Assault ☐   Joy riding ☐   Shoplifting ☐
   Theft ☐   Vandalism ☐   Other crime/s ☐
   Mugging ☐   Graffiti ☐

5. Do you know someone else who has been involved in crime?
   Yes ☐   No ☐

6. Do you think it is worthwhile getting involved in crime?
   Yes ☐   No ☐

7. What is the reason for your answer? _____

8. Why do you think young people get involved in crime?
   Boredom ☐   Excitement ☐
   Pressure from friends ☐   Other reason ☐

9. Do you think young people are worried about going to prison?
   Yes ☐   No ☐

10. Do you think more should be done to reduce/prevent crime?
    Yes ☐   No ☐

11. What do you think needs to be done? _____

20 Accessing ... Citizenship: Crime and Justice

What punishment?

Activity 1: Word search

Find the answers to the clues in the word search. Use the images in the Student Book on pages 22 and 23 to help you.

g	i	b	b	e	t	i	r	o	n	s	y	n	s
h	s	h	m	t	s	v	a	n	j	l	o	a	c
h	b	m	l	k	k	j	h	g	f	d	s	a	a
f	l	a	z	c	b	n	m	j	l	p	m	b	f
c	i	d	v	b	x	b	v	e	f	y	h	u	f
b	f	h	t	q	a	j	j	e	w	u	p	z	o
m	e	p	m	u	t	r	e	a	d	m	i	l	l
o	l	l	i	j	a	g	s	h	i	e	w	l	d
p	p	t	c	r	i	m	i	n	a	l	s	m	w
s	u	i	y	l	r	c	s	h	b	n	e	p	s
t	r	e	w	q	f	g	p	i	h	g	i	r	a
o	y	f	c	v	n	l	c	h	t	r	a	i	s
c	s	o	g	u	m	a	n	a	c	l	e	s	a
k	a	d	g	l	o	t	h	u	p	w	o	o	m
s	h	a	c	k	l	e	s	y	d	r	i	n	b
p	c	i	d	s	r	a	f	h	b	z	m	o	l
p	u	n	i	s	h	e	d	h	p	m	u	t	p

Clues:

1 Criminals were put in these and had rotten vegetables thrown at them.
2 The body of a hanged criminal was shown to the public in these.
3 Prisoners had to do at least 50 steps a minute on this.
4 Criminals were hanged from this.
5 A type of handcuffs used in the twelfth century.
6 Chains that were put around a prisoner's ankles in the twelfth century.
7 If you commit a crime you will be sent to _____ .
8 A criminal can spend the rest of his/her _____ in prison.
9 The name given to the person who locked up prisoners in the past.
10 If you are caught committing a crime you will be _____ .
11 People who commit crimes are called _____ .

© Folens (copiable page), Accessing ... Citizenship: Crime and Justice

Life behind bars

Activity 1: Star diagram

Look at all the images showing life behind bars on pages 24–25 of the Student Book. Then complete this star diagram by trying to imagine what life in prison must be like and answering these questions.

| What is it like being stuck in a small cell for most of the day? | How does it feel to be in here? | What's it like sharing your cell? |

| What are the other prisoners like? | **Life behind bars** | What are the prison guards like? |

| What is your day-to-day routine? | How often do you get to have visitors? |

Extension activity

Imagine you are in prison. Write a diary describing what your life is like as a prisoner.

Anti-social behaviour orders... is this the way forward?

Information sheet 1: Preston Street Gang

In a rundown area of Brackton, the streets have suddenly become peaceful and happy places once more. Senior citizens and mothers with children are now happy and confident to walk to their local shops again.

This is a dramatic change, from just a few weeks ago, when residents of the area lived in fear of the local 'Preston Street Gang' who terrorised the neighbourhood with their abusive, violent and anti-social behaviour. In an unusual step, the local police force named and shamed the members of the gang – and they are now subject to a mass Anti-social behaviour order, which bans them from the local streets.

How do the locals feel? Most of the local people questioned would only respond if their identities were kept secret.

It's much quieter now. They used to break windows and spray graffiti everywhere. And they used to spit on my windows. It was disgusting. Every day I had to clean it off. It made me feel sick.

The gang were involved in drugs and were regularly involved in violence. They've been convicted of more than 100 offences between them. However crime has gone down by 25% since the ASBOs went out.

My wife wouldn't put the bins out at night, she was so scared. And the old lady next door used to ask me to walk down to the shops with her, in case that gang was about.

Even if they weren't actually doing anything, they would intimidate people just by hanging around outside the shops. They terrorised people by just being there.

The results have been dramatic. It is so much quieter now. I am just glad they were removed peacefully.

Anti-social behaviour orders... is this the way forward?

Information sheet 2: Preston Street Gang

We're going to take the council to court and challenge this. Our family life has been ruined.

We've torn down as many of the posters as we could. It's not right treating people like this.

This may be a relief, but the likelihood is that it is a temporary fix rather than a solution to a problem.

It's quite clearly important to respond to anti-social behaviour and to be seen to respond to it. There is no doubt people who are on the receiving end of it wish for something to be done.

Anti-social behaviour orders... is this the way forward?

Activity 1: What do you think? Write your answers in the boxes.

1 Do you think the residents of Brackton are happy with the ASBO?

2 Why do you think they were only willing to give their opinion if they didn't have to give their names?

3 Do you think the mothers of the gang members have the 'right' to ask local people to sign their petition?

4 How would you feel if one of the mothers asked you to sign the petition? Would you sign it?

5 Do you think anti-social behaviour orders (ASBOs) are a good idea?

6 Will ASBOs 'solve' the problems experienced by the community in Brackton?

7 Do you think the *Daily News*' 'Dob on a yob' campaign is good idea?

8 Can you think of other ways to tackle anti-social behaviour?

Extension activity
Find out if there are any similar anti-social behaviour order schemes operating in your local area.

Is there justice?

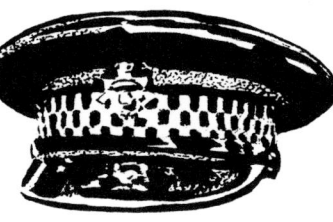

It is difficult being a police officer. Victims of crime want immediate results, but this is not always possible. But can the police make things better for the victims of crime?

Activity 1: Heroes and villains

Look at the four stories in the Student Book on pages 28–31.

1 Which stories show the police 'positively'?

2 Which stories show the police 'negatively'?

3 In the stories in which the police seem to have been 'unhelpful', can you make suggestions as to how the police could have handled the situation differently?

Suggestions to the police in story ...	Suggestions to the police in story ...

© Folens (copiable page), Accessing … Citizenship: Crime and Justice

The Howard League for Penal Reform

Activity 1: Who was John Howard?

You'll find some of the answers to the following questions in the Student Book, but you will also have to do some research to answer all the questions.

Write your answers on a clean sheet of paper.

1 When was John Howard born?

2 Where was he born?

3 Why did he become interested in the prison system?

4 What is the name of the book he wrote?

5 Why was a statue built of him in St Paul's Cathedral?

6 Can you find a famous quote from him?

7 When did he die?

8 When was the Howard League for Penal Reform created?

9 How does the organisation get its money?

Are there any other questions you would like to ask to be able to find out more about John Howard?

Accessing ... Citizenship: Crime and Justice

The Howard League for Penal Reform

Activity 1: Investigating campaigns

Working in small groups, use the project planning guide on page 31 to find out more about the work of the Howard League for Penal Reform. First choose one of the campaigns highlighted in the Student Book.

the **Howard League** for **Penal Reform**

The campaign we are going to investigate is …	We want to investigate this campaign because …
Through the investigation we hope to find out … (write down some questions you would like to find the answers to).	The campaign logo looks like this … (If the campaign you have chosen doesn't have a logo, design one here.)

Now use all the information you have gathered to create a display about the campaign. Use suitable pictures, graphs, quotes or headline facts to make your display more eye-catching and interesting. You will present your work to the rest of the class.

We got our information about the campaign from …

© Folens (copiable page), Accessing … Citizenship: Crime and Justice

Is there an alternative? ... Focus on Grendon Prison

Activity 1: Ideas of home

Look at the boxes from the artwork installation at Grendon shown in the Student Book on page 35. Look at the items the prisoners have chosen. Why do you think they have chosen these items? Write your answers in this table.

Box	Reason
Razor	
Quilt	
Drinking straw	
Child's drawing	
Photograph	
Pencil case	

Activity 2: My home

What would you put or draw in your box and why?

This is what represents my home to me:

I have chosen this image because …

The Youth Justice System

Find the phrase

Complete the grid below with the answers to these clues. The letters in boxes will form a phrase running down the page.

1. Another word for a young person.
2. One of the aims of the Youth Justice System is to encourage …
3. The person who calls the witness to court and keeps the public out.
4. Another aim of the Youth Justice System is to encourage …
5. The person responsible for a young offender's health.
6. One of the new bodies created to deal with young people who commit crime.
7. The person responsible for the young offender's learning.
8. The person responsible for looking after the young offender and writing reports.
9. The person responsible for supervising the offender after they have been to court and helping the police.
10. The third aim of the Youth Justice System is to encourage …
11. The person responsible for charging and recording the offence at the 'station'.
12. This person 'keeps an eye' on the work of the Youth Offending Teams.
13. A young person might break the law to get money to buy these.
14. If a young person is found guilty they can be sent here.
15. A person who tells the court what happened because they were there and saw the offence.
16. A young person who keeps breaking the law will end up here.
17. A young person may break the law because of this, if they can't find anything better to do.
18. The person who decides whether the young person is guilty or not.

1. ☐ _ U _ _
2. _ _ _ _ _ _ _ ☐ _ _ _ _ _ _ _ _ _ Y
3. _ _ _ ☐ _ H _ _ _
4. _ _ _ ☐ _ _ _ _ _ _ N
5. ☐ _ _ _ _ _ _ W _ _ _ _ _ _
6. Y _ _ _ _ ☐ _ _ _ _ _ _ _ _ _ B _ _ _ _
7. _ D ☐ _ _ _ _ _ _ _ W _ _ _ _ _ _
8. ☐ _ _ _ L _ _ _ K _ _
9. _ _ _ B _ ☐ _ _ _ _ F _ _ _ _ _ _
10. _ _ ☐ _ T _ _ _ _ _ _ _ _ _
11. _ _ L _ ☐ _ _ _ _ _ _ _ _ _ R
12. _ _ M ☐ S _ _ _ _ _ _ _ _
13. _ _ _ _ G ☐
14. ☐ _ _ _ G _ _ _ _ N _ _ _ _ _ _ S _ _ _ _ _ _ _ _ _ _
15. _ _ _ _ _ _ S ☐
16. _ O _ _ ☐
17. _ _ _ _ ☐ D _ _
18. ☐ _ G _ _ _ _ _ _ _

Use the all the pages in the Student Book about young offenders to help you work out the answers.

The phrase is … _____

Preventing crime

Activity 1: How can you prevent crime?

List the different ways that you can help prevent crime. The pictures on pages 46 and 47 of the Student Book may help you.

Where	How
At home	
Personal belongings/ safety	
In your community	
At school	
In vehicles including bikes	
Other places?	

Activity 2: Raising awareness of crime prevention

Do you think it is important to raise awareness of crime prevention?

Design a poster or leaflet to inform other people in your school or local community how they can help to prevent crime, for example, by raising awareness of getting personal possessions marked with a special pen. Use the images in the Student Book to give you ideas.

Want to know more?

Write a project about an issue which interests you from the Student Book.

Activity 1: How can you prevent crime?

Before you start, spend some time working out how you are going to organise your project. Read through the following stages and think about your answers for each one. Then you should be able to write a plan for your project. Page 32 will also help you.

Step 1: choose a topic you are interested in

It is important to have a clear focus for your project. Your teacher can help you decide. Look through the Student Book to get some ideas.

Step 2: take your time to narrow your focus

You may have to narrow the focus of the project. Think of a title that says exactly what you are looking at, or a question you would like to answer.

Examples: topic: victims of crime
           focus: victim support
           question: which organisations support victims of crime?

Step 3: do not rely on one source of information

Try to find information from a variety of sources.

The internet is a useful place to find information about different organisations and issues. You could try using some of the web addresses on page 48 of the Student Book to find useful information. You may be able to email organisations directly to find out more information from them.

Printed sources: books, magazines and newspapers may also cover your topic.

Step 4: break up your text with titles, graphs and pictures

Do not just copy all the useful information you find. Think about how the information helps you to answer the question you set at the beginning of the project. How can you present the information?

Step 5: drawing a conclusion

At the end of the project, try to sum up what you have discovered. This is the place where you have to say what you think about the topic. Remember to give your reasons for your opinions.

© Folens (copiable page), Accessing ... Citizenship: Crime and Justice

Accessing ... Citizenship: Crime and Justice

Want to know more?

Writing your project

Use the planning guide to help you write your project

Name | Class

My topic is:

The focus of my project is:

Sources of information:

How I am going to organise the information:

Illustrations, etc. I am going to use:

My conclusion/What have I discovered?